# The Son of
the Duke
of Nowhere

## PHILIP GROSS

*faber and faber*

LONDON · BOSTON

First published in 1991
by Faber and Faber Limited
3 Queen Square London WC1N 3AU

Photoset by Wilmaset Birkenhead Wirral
Printed in England by
Clays Ltd, St Ives plc

© Philip Gross, 1991

A CIP record for this book is available from the British Library

ISBN 0-571-16140-5

Acknowledgements are due to the following magazines and anthologies: *The
Listener, London Magazine, New Statesman & Society, Poetry Book Society
Anthology 1988–89, Poetry Book Society Anthology 1989–90, Poetry London,
Poetry Review, Spectator, Stand.*

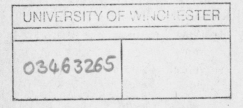

## The Son of the Duke of Nowhere

Philip Gross was born in 1952, in Delabole, Cornwall. His father was a Displaced Person from Estonia; his mother was Cornish. After studying English at Sussex University, he worked in publishing and libraries before moving to Bristol. He now divides his time between writing, poetry work in schools and colleges, and his own two children.

*The Ice Factory* was published by Faber and Faber in 1984. *Cat's Whisker* (Faber, 1987) was a Poetry Book Society Recommendation and *The Air Mines of Mistila*, a verse-fable written with Sylvia Kantaris (Bloodaxe, 1988), a Poetry Book Society Choice. He won a Gregory Award in 1981 and the National Poetry Competition in 1982; his first radio play, *Internal Affairs*, shared the prize in the BBC West of England Playwriting Competition 1986. His first collection of poems for children, *Manifold Manor*, appeared in 1989, and a novel for young people, *The Song of Gail and Fludd*, was published in spring 1991. He received a major Arts Council bursary in 1989 for his work for young people.

# Contents

# Welcome to the Forest

For a thirty-sixth birthday

So here it is: the walled-up door
only visible at certain
shifts of light, the door the stories
mentioned. Now it opens
for you; one step and you're somewhere

else. That cats-and-cabbage smell,
the murk, the sinking
underfoot, the rising damp you feel
in your bones say: this is
it, not a figure of speech, this is all

the forest there is. Here's an armchair
unbuttoned like Falstaff,
a snakepit of bedsprings, some lovers'
burst balloon, a single
small red welly, and a dumped Cortina

drifted deep in leaf-mould. You're just
passing through. (That's
what they all said.) And you're almost
sure of the path until
it twists again. And whom do you trust:

the woodman whistling through his teeth
    as he buffs up his axe?
Or the wolf-boy who comes sidling out
    to lay a clutch of pignuts
and a snared thrush dumbly at your feet?

# Away from it All

He tried to write home
again, then crunched in the mist down the shingle,
out past a pillbox burying itself backwards

like a crab. He went stooped
as if hunting the one perfect globe of a stone
that must exist somewhere. The sea got up uncombed

with a scurf of rusty scud
and polystyrene. He was listening for the stream
that would burst up through the pebbles with a roar

come Spring, the locals said.
Even they had been making themselves scarcer
like the hours of daylight. The only trace

of any other life was the mould
on the mixed-fruit jam, *Five go to Devil's Island*,
and a book of crosswords, half-done, wrong.

The gas had puttered out
days since with a whiff of fish. He lay in silence
scoured by the all-night traffic of the waves,

and woke to a shudder of flight,
was it, once, overhead, then the flat wonk
of a goose come adrift from its squadron.

He had wanted to write:
*I'm free as the wind here, nothing to distract*
*me from . . . from . . .* The paper stayed as blank

as the mist that shifted blind
on blind, and suddenly was alive with nothing
he could see: a quivering hum, a slap of tackle,

whickering taut wires . . .
A flock of white sails beat by, white-blind,
feeling their way home along the shore.

# Son of Snotnose

### for J.K.G.

*tattnina* (Estonian): a small oil lamp, literally 'snotnose'

There's a smutty flicker
on two crescent faces:
one, a woman hauled up
in her ninth month; one, a maid
who fusses at a wick

that drips, drips.
'Stop your cackling, child!'
In the stung hush
something up the hillside
crackles and spits

like brush-wood
catching fire. Now again
a lumbering crunch. The flame
jinks. Then
'It's stopped.' Across the yard

hens ruffle and subside.
'What now?' Drip,
drip. They're still,
so still,
that when the door kicks wide,

it's he who hangs amazed,
the enemy, the uninvited
guest, swaying in
towards their light,
one fist half raised

but trembling, rifle
slung askew, that shallow
Tartar face . . . A boy,
half way to dead and knows
it, and how many miles

from home. No one
can move. He stares and stares
till the thud of a shell
rattles the shutters.
Then he ducks and runs.

A wrenched hinge creaks.
A squat flame trips
in the draught. The snotnose
drips.
When the woman speaks

it's a rusty whisper: 'Quick.
Get water. Wedge the door.
Help me . . .' It is 1919
and not much else is clear.
'And for God's sake trim that wick!'

# The Duke of Nowhere

I was the son of the Duke of Nowhere.
Nowhere was home. The first sound I remember

was engines sawing steam, the butt
and squeal of waggons full of clunk

shunted cruelly. Lifted to the window-sill
I had my first sight of our exile

as I thought: *Here, me,*
*watching. There, trains, going away.*

\*

He was living incognito
but his secret was safe with me.

I was the solitary heir to everything
he never once mentioned. I guessed,

from his brooding, his whole silent days,
it must be vast. The lost estates

grew vaster in the weeks,
then months, he went away and stayed.

\*

Beyond the roofs, beyond the dockyard wall
were cranes, then the edge of the world.

On a clear day I could watch grey frigates
climb it and slip over. I woke one night

to singing in the streets that suddenly
grew small as all the hooters of the fleet

brawled up together, blurting
*Home* . . . as if any such place

existed, over the horizon, anywhere.

# Lahti

## I

. . . the child won't sleep,
does it to spite us, you'd think
there was no one in the whole world but him,

even when we're alone
what do we do but argue about *him*,
we never just sit and not talk now, we can't begin,

and that's without the endless
calling – '*Just this once . . .*' – night
after night – '*I'll never ask again . . .*' – the same lie,

we put a stop to that,
but now he creeps, the child gets out
and *prowls*, just when we get quiet on the sofa there's

a creak on the stairs,
that's why I keep the wireles on, Light
Programme, but I hear, I can't stop myself listening,

thinking *Where is he now*, God knows where it'll end . . .

There are no wolves in England.

Not on the landing
or the long downstairs.
Not in the kitchen

where the lino glistens
like dark ice.
Not in the yard

behind the toolshed
or the toilet door.
There's nothing

in the shadows of the trees
but shadows.
Everybody knows

the wolves are gone,
gone limping
off across the snow,

so far from anywhere.
However many
there may seem to be

each one
sits singly
and their howls

only lengthen the night between them.

3

It was built like a miniature Odeon
in wood veneer. It had a cheeky dial
that blushed when it was on. The grille
at the back showed valves that hummed

in their own dimmed cathedral glow.
*Uncle Mac's Children's Favourites* was OK
but when no one was looking I tuned to Lahti
and caught the sound of snow

or sometimes a faint howling. Night
after night I haunted the landing. A band
of warmth would glow under the door
I never could open. I thought they might

pick up the signal. But I was too far
north, in Lahti. They were in some private
south with Perry Como. *Magic Moments*,
he sang. *Catch a Falling Star . . .*

# A Summit in Slovenia

Miles down, the Jesenice steelworks broils
but we find last year's snow still dossing
wrapped in pine-mess, a tramp in a sack.
The trees all wear hair shirts of lichen.
A cloud moves through the wood. Dull bells

of drop-eared sheep nod by. A cuckoo
mocks itself. Somewhere up in the mist
is a line where the mountains trade names
like small change. There's a frontier post
and peaked caps, but the cloud slips through.

In a roadside hut, the man behind the bar
pilots his radio dial to catch the news
in any of five languages. All are scrambled
by a sound like crumbling scree. Too
far above it all, our reception is poor.

Out in the woods, the ants are building empires,
ziggurats of dead wood, towers of Babel.
They need only a flagpole; I plant my stick.
Hundreds swarm up. At the top, they wave
then blunder back, wagging antennae: *Brothers,*

*turn back! There has been some mistake . . .*

# The Painter of the Lake

He slaps a quick grey drench
across the sky. As it weeps
he works his colours in,

old man with misty glasses
and a little box of tricks
that folds out neat bright tinctures.

A crowd begins to gather, shyly:
children, dogs, then half
the village at a little distance.

Our lake, our two mountains.
He gives them back to us
perfect. Every Sunday afternoon.

He makes them as they are.
He washes out his brushes
in the lake, which is why

it keeps its blue-green-grey,
year in, year out.
Only today

he has not come. Instead,
your coach arrives scattering
the goats. Your faces gaze

from its green-smoked glass
like carp. Our children
find their own reflections

in your hubcaps. But
the painter? Is he ill?
Oh, if he dies

what will you make of us?

# Saying When

Was it *then*, as we stopped by the river
watching our charmed blur shiver off downstream
towards the crushed sound of the weir?

Was it then that the world
became less than it was: she died,
in a room above deep gardens that grew wild

by night, the houses dark beyond, a postage stamp
of window lit maybe to frame
a single head, a lamp?

Was that when one more country became nowhere
on the map, with its cafés, its spas
weeping condensation, its grey commissionaires

in chocolate coats with stiff gold tassels?
Uniforms were innocent as plumage;
years piled lightly as the flakes of strudels

she force-fed guests . . . Those, and powdery
moon-shaped biscuits, sinister
with almonds. 'Let the boy eat!'

she would cry. She had a sweet decaying smell,
cut flowers. 'Let him eat while he can.
Who can tell?'

Was it *then*,
when all at once you shivered:
'Let's go home'? Or when

a haze off the river rose up like a swan
into our headlights? I swerved but it was nothing,
and no sooner seen than gone.

# Sunspots

He took an interest in the sun,
all its flare-ups and foibles,
like an uncle
with no children of his own.

With his Captain Pugwash spyglass,
he brought it down, neat
as a tea-cup on a linen tablecloth.
*See*, he said, *there's one!*

More like a fly-smut, I thought. Or
a tea-leaf. *That's a storm,*
he said, *the diameter*
*of the earth*. He notched

another on his chart.
*There's a rhythm to them,*
*gives us earthquakes, floods,*
*God knows. Not*

*that it means a jot or tittle*
*to the sun*. All the while
he fussed at the focus.
It was never quite clear.

It might have been
somebody's fortune in the leaves
or a biopsy slide.
That speck, there . . .

And another, here . . .

*Envoi*

for S.M.K. – 11.9.88

There was a high green after-sunset
like an empty picture palace
dimming to a glow

before the main feature.
Nothing. Space.
And the hills folding in for the night

and a small plane
rising, an X-
marks-the-spot silhouette

that dissolved
between one glance and the next,
the wing-lights moving on.

It was nothing to do with you.
No sign, no metaphor.
It was nothing beyond

itself: a small
plane rising as down in the dark
I watched and you

were dead. But for a moment
it seemed clear: there was space
to hold us. That was all.

I would have liked to tell you.

# Plainsong

Whacked up in a gust,
it stoops: a hawk? No,
it's a black bin-bag —

one of the gale's jokes
as it bullies through
the park. Safe inside

I can trace the four-
square shape of our walls
edged in wind as you

speak of somebody's
child who is dying.
Now I can hear you

breathing, we're so still.

*

There's a lot more sky
this morning after.
The last of the elms,

laid out, has jacked up
a ten-foot divot
fuzzed with torn root-hairs

like fused nerves. Children
whoop out of doors high,
jumpy with static,

to swarm the shivered
timbers. The littlest,
left behind, stares down

into the fresh pit.

*

Now the chain-saw gang
begins its nasal
plainsong in the park.

A shattered slate waits
slap on the doorstep
like today's papers –

STORM KILLS THREE (there but
for the grace of . . .) Who
smudged this black thumb-print

on the weather map,
contour lines so steep
only children dare

run down them, laughing?

# The Ark

Spindly in a heat haze, almost out of sight,
the boy comes to the edge. A peevish ripple
dries on the hard sand at his feet. The tide
   stalls at a dead point between pull

and push. It seems an age. He turns his back
on the brightly huddled bivouac of his family
up the dunes. He won't hear when (*if*, he thinks)
   they call. It is summer, 1963

and he spends it pacing like a lookout on a border
that won't stay still. Somewhere the sea folds back
into sky but he can't see the join. The surface
   blisters like paint. Something black

marks the one fixed point: the mast-tip
of a torpedoed tanker. It's lain twenty years
down there, slimed, encrusting, only glimpsed
   at the lowest of ebbs. He shivers

in the heat. One more push, the sea might slide
right off like a blanket and the wreck rise
tall as an ark on a desert of shrivelling weed.
   And then the flies.

# Frost Fair

        fires on the ice
        tonight's the night
    for fighting cock and baited bull and dancing bear
        men swallowing swords
        and tugs of war
    and everyone who's anyone is there

*we're talking entertainment now  we're talking the big show*
*we're talking tricks and treats  we're talking kicks*
*we're talking the now scene  talking like there's no tomorrow*
*we're talking pleasure cruises on the River Styx*

        fires on the ice
        tonight's the night
    there's everything to sell and none to spare
        and everything's more
        than we can afford
    we'll blow the lot tonight and we won't care

*we're talking business now  we're talking the big deal*
*we're talking quick bucks  talking Futures  talking Gilts*
*we're talking Big Bang  talking big risks  talking the Big Wheel*
*we're talking greasy poles and dwarfs on stilts*

        fires on the ice
            tonight's the night
    there's red smoke rising in the glassy air
            the ice may creak
            beneath our feet
    we'll dance with frost and ashes in our hair


    *we're talking bigshots  bigwigs  talking pride before the Fall*
    *we're talking tightrope walkers  strongmen  quacks*
    *we're talking walking on the water  talking anything at all*
    *we're talking hopscotch  don't step on the cracks*


        fires on the ice
            tonight's the night
    for preachers peddling their whys and wares
            the hall of mirrors
            house of horrors
    and the eyes out in the dark that stare
                                    and stir

# Threads

Yes, but what about the spiders? There'll be no
   sheds, pelmets, crannies under stairs,
     no room for supercargo
   in the bunkers, whose conditioned air
will certainly exclude flies. Where will they go?

*Seven years' bad luck, to kill a spider* . . . (Yes.
   Just one.) How many species of *arachnidae*,
     how many money-spinners,
   mummy-swaddlers, house-guests, high-
wire-walkers, air-fishers, scuttlers, secret sharers?

How many threads to pick up? A small brocaded bead
   sewn into her work, she makes the pattern
     new each day, Eve's-
   dropper, bag-woman, common-or-garden
Dame *Diademata*. She taps into tingling wires to read

all the news that's fit to eat. She's a radio-astronomer
   sifting the hum of space; here's the slight
     bleat of a quasar,
   the crumpling of a sun, a distant *Try*
*try try again* . . .
                Today, a first stiffening of the air,

and the webs touched in white on the privet . . . Such
   glass bead games, such Honiton lace,
      such moon-dust.
   But empty; the pattern was lost,
for this year at least. They would crumble at my touch.

## Petit Mal

Just a flutter
   behind your eyes,
     a swirl of snow

that melts at my touch
   and you wonder why I ask
     *Where did you go?*

*What's happening?*
   'Nothing,' you say.
     It's nothing, true:

a tiny death?
   a leaving home?
     Who knows? Not you.

Not the feverish script
   writ by the moving
     finger of the EEG.

Not the maze-mandalas,
   shadow-maps,
     that are all I see

in the brain-scan
   negatives. No trace
     of the gusts of flight

or free fall
   I've felt brush
      past me to light

wing-quivering
   on your skin, as if
      to mark you out. So

slight. So hard
   to hold you. Harder still
      to let you go.

# What the Mountain Saw

They arrive by night, travel-stunned, and see nothing.
They sleep wrapped in pine-tang and the rush of waters.
The father is first awake. He clacks the shutters back
and a mountain squats square at the window, looking in.

It never leaves them, though it changes hour by hour,
twisting a scarf of cloud, or turning a hard profile
to the morning sun, or dissembling a sugar-pink haze.
However far they walk – and they walk, walk every day –

it's above them, a bit of beyond. Some snow hangs on
in shreds. This is a famous north face, and a killer.
Each day the father scans it with his old binoculars
for any hint of tracks, and never finds them.

So the holiday proceeds, in a series of snapshots.
Here, in mid-stride, he crests a rise, wife and child
at his boot-heels, tranced by their thud and the heat
and the insect hum. But the snow-face is no nearer.

Here, through veils of spruce, he breaks into a glade
possessed by pallid green-veined hellebores.
Or here, he brings the family, breathless, to its knees
before one icicle-white wild crocus. Here is the lake

he finds them, like a souvenir, round and still
enough to hold the mountain, till a fish jumps.
In between, there are the hours he drives them on
for health. Stop too long, the sweat begins to chill.

'*Breathe deep!*' he cries, and strikes out higher
up a wide white stony stream-bed, tumbled and scoured
by the spring melt, strewn with tree-trunks, torn
and bleached, and a few tiny tough mauve flowers

he can't name. He grips the child's hand as she teeters
on a plank beneath a waterfall. Its ice-breath touches them.
Their hair goes white with spray. Afterwards he will say
'*That was our furthest point,*' and sigh. As they drag home

footsore, the mountain shows itself again behind them,
in its pure dream of itself, untouched . . . Just as now
it looks in through the breakfast-room window when the child,
as if the strings that control her had fouled

and were jerked tight, has one of her turns. An egg
tips from its silver cup, a glass pirouettes to the edge
but has not yet smashed, the other guests have not
yet turned to stare, the father reaches for her but

is frozen. He will never reach her. Any moment now
the yolk will burst on crisply laundered linen. Soon
there will be splinters and tears. Behind it all he sees
the mountain at the window. *If one could stand there*

*looking down*, he thinks, *this would all be very small.*

# The Dancing Princesses

It was an age of ballgowns: antique whims
she dredged up barnacled with gems.

Day in, day out she drew them, her exquisite
dummies. How could they dance? Hands and feet

were afterthoughts. And their perfectly lovely
empty faces last of all, their eyes only

for her. Unfluttering, they stared her through
and through. They would not let her go

till they'd taken one year of her ten.
Then something hidden by the gowns began

to connect, hand to foot. To move, before
my eyes. To dance. We are not what we were.

No more king, no princesses . . . The last
of her line furls a billow of scarlet,

quick as something going up in flames.
And there, arm locked to her waist,

is a thin man, all in black,
stiff as a stake. His back

is to me. I can't see his face.

# The End of the Line

They sit as far apart as you can in a small compartment.

Their windows run different channels. The girl's shows the
works: vats stickered with HAZCHEM signs, pipes thick as
sewers, thin stilt-walking pipes, glinty capillaries. Among
them is waste. The day shift has been swallowed without
trace. A box, a bicycle, a body even, could lie about for
days.

One chimney leaks a fleecy white, one a thin slick of crocus
yellow. The fumes do not rise but stretch out tethered,
thinning. Yeah, thinks the girl, I sort of like it.

The woman's window shows a brown sullen sweep of estuary.
It glitters, just: light weighs it down like silt. There is a long
decline of glossy mud, worm-pimpled, gulched with rivulets.
Wading birds, spick black and white like waiters, hitch their
thin legs at the train's clack and flicker away.

Across it lies a see-through shadow, the reflection of the girl.
Silly child, thinks the woman. Done up in black like a crone
in mourning. And that carefully dishevelled hair, the tarry
eyes, the china-clay pallor. She wants to be noticed, just to
throw it back. Silly child. And yet.

The woman looks straight now. Yes, beneath it all, a face, not
pretty, not plain, and for a moment not thinking about itself.
Little girl, there's trouble there; your chin comes up, slightly,
to meet it. Why do your lips clinch? Under that sloe-stain

lipstick they would be pale. Why make me notice you? I want to be alone.

She looks too long. The girl turns. Which of them will speak?

There is no one else. A few disembarked at the works, stragglers to offices or odd shifts, maybe. No one got on, and why should they? There is one more stop, the Beach. No one goes there. It is inhabited but no one goes. It is the end of the line.

One of us should apologize, the woman thinks. Me, for staring? You, for . . . just being like that? And being *here*. Do your parents know? But the girl's eyes give nothing, no sooner there than somewhere else, out of the window. The woman turns back to the mud light of the sea.

\*

The platform is a concrete slab. The track stops without buffers, just like that. Six feet beyond, someone has chanced a row of runner beans in the sand. WAY OUT is a gate-frame with a sentry box. The box is empty; there is no gate; indeed, there is no fence. The woman pauses, ticket vaguely proffered. The girl, who has none, skips by.

And now? If either of them needed to be alone, this is desperate. She would have to stride for twenty minutes up the straight long shore to be out of sight. She would have to pass the shuttered ice-cream booth, the leaning phone box and how very many hardboard chalets with their hand-tooled nameplates: *Sea-View*, *Mon Repos*, *Yertiz*, *Tir Na Nog* . . .

[33]

Two figures in a landscape. Oh dear, thinks the woman. I don't believe it, the girl thinks, Jesus!

The small train shuffles off. With its tactless yellow markings, it is the larval form of something off to pupate or die. As it twitches in among the works and out of sight, the woman wonders what in the world she, or anything at all, is doing here. The emptiness of home, the breakfast room with no children's clutter, no man's moods to disorder it, all that seems vivid by comparison. She surprises herself. She laughs.

The girl turns. Did she hear right? If that was a laugh, it has been swabbed efficiently away. But the woman hasn't moved. She should have been off down her little trodden track to her burrow and out of sight. But no. It isn't her place either.

Should be, though. It's where they come to die. Each hut has an aerial, and a little window-box. They tidy themselves away. Convenient. And this one? Not old, not a granny quite, but dithery. Dry dowdy little thing – no, not drab, quite neat in a plain way, like a little bird in earth colours, dust colours, camouflage. Careful.

Yes, careful. Something in the way she keeps her face, fine stress-lines holding up the smile. She copes. She's a worrier. In a minute she'll be worrying about *me*. Just let her try. And at once the girl pulls back: anxious old bat, schoolteacher most like, and a virgin, dried up, done for. The girl's black eye-slits narrow. Beats me, she thinks, people like her. Why don't they just jack it in?

But the woman does an odd thing. She squats down. On a late, bruised-looking roadside weed, a butterfly quivers. That's all I need, the girl thinks, nature study! As if knocked sideways by the violence of her scorn, the Cabbage White staggers off. Its flight-path lifts her eyes beyond the huts to those chimneys and their urine-coloured stain. That'll do for you, she thinks with satisfaction, you'll turn black, or you'll mutate into something horrid. She relaxes into a familiar story: mutants, great! The Beasts From Planet X. Dead good. I'm a mutant myself, you know, little lady. Must be something in the water. Your lot haven't got a clue.

The woman glances up, catches a smile on the girl's face and, why not, smiles back.

*

The sea wall is a massive sandbagging of limestone blocks. Without it the estuary's fifty-foot tides would have dispensed with this spit of shingle long ago. As it is, they slick past, baffled, churning at the point.

The woman sits heavily. Her age is telling her something. One hand smooths the white stone, picking at the prints of fossils, absently. Detritus of crushed shells, perfect rings of snapped crinoids. Sea lilies, combing long hair on the currents. Little life forms superseded, obsolete. Mute silt. Tiny lives.

'Oh I do love to be beside the seaside.' As if she has sensed this fit of philosophy coming on, the girl kicks off black boots and white, shockingly childish, ankle socks. She hitches up her skirt and dances down the boulders to the mud. The woman wonders if the show is meant for her. The child becomes so small so quickly.

Now she is at the mud, picking her feet up high, ickily delighted by the stick and slide of it. The tide is slooshing in, stretching long smooth contours round the point. A sitting gull rides by. There is a pool of dead unpolished water in the lee. At its edge, little swirls break free and fight back against the flow, black eyelets of whirlpools drifting off, filling and fading. She is in past her knees.

The woman is very still. Does she imagine it, or does the girl turn and squint back to the shore? Does the girl imagine it, or is that old bag still watching her? The girl's face sets: just let her try . . . I could show her. She wades deeper. Her hem slips and is sodden. She feels a vibration like a dull beat. Just ahead, the surface wakes in a hushed lithe turbulence. The water is abruptly cold.

The woman gets up, suddenly. For a moment her neck stiffens to shout, her legs tense to attempt the boulders. Then she turns away. You can't hold her, she thinks, you can't hold anyone. Let go, she wills the fingers cramped into her palms, let go. Now, look, I *hope* you're looking, here I am, walking away.

*

The train is a minute or two late. The woman hears feet slap up the concrete behind her, just in time. What can she do but turn? What does one say?

'OK?' she ventures. And the girl, with a slightest of nods, seals their compact: 'OK.'

# On the Hoof

Sweet musk
of sweat and chips and petrol.
Sunglassed cabin cruisers lie

at anchor like a sneer of perfect teeth.
The waves slope off
smudging fingerprints of diesel.

One last toddler pokes
in a pickle of weed,
collecting bits of crab

to build one of his own and
*Shark, Mummy, shark!*
A stiff

rubbery cosh
of a dogfish, ditched,
too small for sport or meat.

The child is smacked.
The gulls come sidling . . .

Now
the front lights up. I cruise
the menus. I approve

the mushroom quiche and salads
you and I might choose
together, then move down

to the Char-Grill-Bar-B-Q.
I've got to eat
and fast. Tonight,

two hundred miles from home,
I feel like meat . . .

The Big Bang Disco flickers.
It's a heart
that suddenly begins to beat.

The lads are all edgy with style.
The girls wear hungry midriffs
bare this year. A bouncer

with a knuckleduster jawline
counts them in
and they're skittish but meek

to his touch: warm bodies,
shuffling feet,
nudging on down the narrowing chute,

the way flesh does:
not grass, but meat . . .

[38]

# Beach Days with Bunker

*The father's on hands and knees*
*slapping buttresses up.*
*The waves are yapping at his heels.*

*One smooths the curve of the wall.*
*The man frowns round*
*at the boy has been no help at all,*

*dribbling mud into slim knobbly spires*
*with the devotion of an icon painter.*
*There's a lull while breakers*

*(no white horses, these,*
*but grey stocky steppe ponies)*
*muster. Now a big push creams*

*up the breastwork. The horde pours in,*
*over, on each other's shoulders*
*and a crack sags a foolish grin,*

*bulwarks begin to slump and liquefy*
*though the father's still slabbing away.*
*They dissolve in his hands with a sigh.*

*And the boy? He's watching, simply watching.*

\*

You report to your parents punctually
on the hour. You've found a rockpool

with strawberry jellies in it
and a friend. Is it lunchtime yet?

That's nice, they say. And, no. And,
who? They tilt their shades and frown

the way you point, but can't see,
it's the glare. So off you run.

Bunker's waiting on a rock. 'What
did I tell you?' He teaches you to poke

the pink anemones and make them pucker.
Your fingertip recalls their tingling

all day, and you juggle your sandwich
with the other hand, for fear of poison.

*

    When Bunker calls
no one looks up. You'd think they were conspiring
    to ignore him.
    Not for long.

    When Bunker smiles
you get this itching all inside your skin.
    Mother lards you with Cool-Tan
    none too gently.

When Bunker laughs,
all the gulls start up and mob off, clanging
      their alarm bells.
      It'll end in tears.

      When Bunker cries
someone will suffer for it.

      You know who.

*

He's got goofed-out teeth and doesn't care.
A slight niff of sock and foreskin.
He'll show you his scab collection any time,

big and crusty as Roman coins. If you're lucky
he'll click one off between his nails.
You can study the pores

traced out in it. A pale hair.
On his knee, the healed skin's shocking
tender pink. He'll wag his grin at any camera,

only when the prints come back he's never there.

*

You limp back, blooded
   with an angry graze
and won't say who did it or dared you.
A rock bit you, that's all.

You doused the wound yourself,
   didn't whimper,
watched the blood-wisps smoulder away
in salt water like smoke on the wind.

\*

*The boy stands on a lifetime's supply*
*of ammunition. Each stone's a snug fit*
*for somebody's fist. So he lets the sea have it,*

*crook-armed, aboriginal slingshot style.*
*The waves keep coming, the suckers,*
*with easy targets. A snout of driftwood wallows*

*at each bonk but won't sink. A jellyfish bag*
*goes down with one gulp. Next, a gout*
*of polystyrene . . . He bombs it again and again.*

*Each time it bursts it multiplies*
*and rides on, indestructible*
*spores of a notion whose time has come.*

# An Incident on the Line

*near Dawlish*

It's the same wet week, the length of England.
Each glistening station-stop depletes a few

till just three of us loll – half doze, half daze.
We've left our faces unattended. A cardboard cup

has been rolling to and fro, tick
tock, since Taunton. There's a thin girl opposite

who sits so tight, the cords of her throat
make an angle with her collarbones.

Her magazine stays shut. She bites her lip
in her sleep; in sleep, her man expands,

his bare arm drapes her like a boa.
Fields of flood slip by where cows and swans

dip into their own reflections.
Dusk draws up mud flats like velvet drapes

to part them in one swish: night,
laced with grapplings of foam. Spray

jounces along the sea wall; a slap of it
smacks the window, combs itself away

in kite-tails, bright milky shudderings.
The slumped man grunts; he shifts his weight

[43]

on the girl. Her eyes open – she's not slept –
to stare over his head, out, where the next

wave bunches and swings for us. She's learning
not to blink. At no one I can see,

she almost smiles . . .

# Dust

Here they come, made of books, made of skin,
   dancing into the breach
between us. They're common as dirt: the least

subspecies of the order *Angel*. Poor things.
   Sunlight uplifts them.
All they want to do is drift and praise.

   But we bother the air
with our clinches and tiffs like electrical storms.
   See how they twitch.

Now I sit and will them: *peace, be still.*
   Your mug of cooling tea
gives up its ghosts. The door slams; bright

   concentric ripples run
into, and shudder through, each other's arms.
   How do weightless

creatures mate? Just now, frisking a cobweb
   idly I brought down
on my head a slow crumbling cloud.

   On its crest something stiff
and silvered surfed at me: the bodiless
   leg-chassis of a spider.

As I flinched, it followed, drawn
   by more than gravity –
the clutch of an old woman in the crowd

with something she just *has* to tell me.

# Heavy Weather

Close. Close as undergrowth.
The air a sweaty animal
that rubbed up against us. Nudged
between us. Close. We tossed
side by side all night, waiting

for something to break. Couldn't touch
for the heat. Even the thunder
kept its distance. Limply
I offered a joke: *the drums,*
*the drums* . . . But you were asleep.

Or pretending. Teasy spats of rain
came and went and couldn't
clear the air. We woke exhausted.
Peeled on clothes that felt rubbery-
damp. Thought: *now what?* Went our ways.

\*

The weather does it. All at once,
all over town, cracks in pavements, patios and walls

boiled over: a thin greasy froth of wings.
The ants rose groggily, fumbling each other in flight,

each pair a fantastical flying machine
of sex that came crashing down. The neuter groundcrew

scrambled. I knelt to watch one queen
on our doorstep, dragging her slim spent male

in the wake of her chariot, still coupled.
They had begun dismantling him. One clutched a wing

overhead in the scrum, like a papery fan
or a dubious bargain from a jumble sale.

# Conspirators

The wine bar is a tastefully
converted catacomb. Framed
by a battery of racked snouts,
the bar girl watches over them
(there's no one else)
with a knowing godmotherly smile
(and she's all of eighteen).

It draws them closer, round a bottle
whose Gothic *Gewürztraumer*
spells like a message in code.
Neither says, *We can't go on
like this*. Because they can.
Still, when they drink
it's to the downfall of the old regime.

Now they'll go home
and pay off the babysitter.
Then they'll tangle with the bedclothes
urgently, as though the four-
in-the-morning knock at the door
might come for them
any moment.

# The Way We Are

### 1

No secrets. Half our lives
together now . . . There's nothing between us
  left unsaid, nothing except . . .

I can't say. If I could
I would pen you a flawless poem, of no lines,
  only spaces. This isn't it.

### 2

A purple flush, almost
a weed . . . It's not till it stiffens
  and parches, going to seed,

that we prize it, tastefully
arranged. Its inscrutable ricepaper faces,
  snuffed lanterns, tethered kites,

fret in a draught too slight
for us to feel, with an itchy sound.
  Dry, everlasting. Honesty.

### 3

So here we are, as if
we had climbed and climbed, on a twisting
    and backsliding scree-track, up

    through hours of mist
       to stop
    and stand together

    at what might be
a crumbling drop – no guide, no view
    and not a word to say.


### 4

    There's a structural fault. Surveyors
frown: 'I'd have built somewhere else if I were you.'
    Cracks, hairline fractures, everywhere

    – in the tired skin of your eyelids,
in the concrete of the yard where our children
    do studious hopscotch (step on a line,

    you're out!) while on the threshold
of another year I hesitate, with this dried bouquet
    and a modest proposal: shall we go on?

### 5

We've plastered it, we've bodged. It opens new each year,
   a fine lightning-track, ceiling to floor.
      It has become familiar

as these creases in our palms, that fork and stutter
   and get crossed; strange voices *will* cut in,
      bills, children, other

calls on our time, squalls of interference. Then
   we hold this old crackling line of pain.
      It connects us again.

### 6

   And if the crash comes? I expect
   to meet you in the rubble, half a brick
in hand. Here's mine. Together, we can build a crack . . .

# A Crumb

As you paused to flick away
one crumb, all you'd been saying, all
I was about to say

deserted me. I saw the tired
skin – sand creased by a flash-flood,
then parched – inside

your elbow, in that place
with no particular name. Erosion,
grain by grain . . . I can't make

you beautiful. It frightens me,
how little we miss, so close. Not a crumb.
What do you see,

and not say, that I deceive myself I hide?

What love can't do
is save us from ourselves, or from each other.
All it *can* do is be true.

# Big Wheel

I touched your hips; I felt your skeleton.
    My finger bones

cupped the hinge of a thigh, the nub of it, so little
    flesh between.

And there I was, in some museum, face to face
    with an exhibit, *Human*,

*Female and Infant:* the clean crib of her pelvis
    empty, and the oh-

so-narrow exit, and the baby's cracked-egg dome,
    a perfect fit.

             And I couldn't let go

like our fling together on the big wheel. Caged
    in cheap thrills

and girders and 100-watt bulbs, the kids screamed
    tirelessly. We watched them

reeling off, weak-kneed, falling into each other's arms.
    Twice their age,

we dared each other to it. The man clinked us in
    without smiling. Threw the switch.

Heavy metal pumped suddenly, swung us up
    in one snatch, juddered,

stopped. We hung in a groundswell of dazzle and dark:
    our big O glittering

its own advertisement across the night, with us, slung
    between creaking bolts,

                    holding on for dear life.

# Catch

*Here is a woman. Here is a man.*
*And here is how the game began.*
*We call it Catch Me if You Can.*


He was the one and only.
           She wrapped him all around.
He kicked against his swaddlings.
           She knew where he was bound.
His first cry was ERGO SUM. She knew the proof was sound.


*I play Robber. You play Cop.*
*We play Catch You on the Hop.*


He toyed with a naked razor.
           She taught him how to shave.
He said: I'm off to do or die.
           She waited like the grave.
He left her on the harbour wall and she became a wave.


*I play Therefore. You play If.*
*We play Try to Catch my Drift.*


He was the lost explorer.
           She was his New Found Land.
He was the pilgrim father.
           She was the shifting sand.
She was the straw he clutched at when he'd nowhere left to stand

*I play Sorry. You play Scold.*
*We play Couldn't Catch a Cold.*

He mused in a country churchyard.
          She was the tongue of the bell.
He prayed to become a hermit.
            She was his spidery cell.
When Heaven left him cold in bed, she was the fires of Hell.

*I play Day. You play Night.*
*We play Catch my Bones Alight.*

He ran away to battle.
          She met him dressed in red.
He won a famous victory.
          She was the wound that bled
and out of it marched the living and into it marched the dead
and there was nothing he could do and no more to be said.

*Here is a woman, here a man*
*and they are nowhere.*
*Peace at last . . .*
              *But*

Is that you?
            Yes. Is that you?
Can we begin again?
            *We can.*